The Ends of the Earth:

Collected Poems

Charles Bane, Jr.

Transcendent Zero Press

Houston, Texas

Copyright © 2015 by Charles Bane, Jr.

PUBLISHED BY TRANSCENDENT ZERO PRESS
www.transcendentzeropress.org

All rights reserved. No part of this book may be reproduced in any format, except as portions used in reviews, without the expressed consent of the publisher and the author.

Transcendent Zero Press
16429 El Camino Real Apt. 7
Houston, Texas 77062

ISBN-10: 0996270418

ISBN-13: 978-0-9962704-1-0

Printed in the United States of America

Library of Congress Control Number: 2015911478

Cover concept: Charles Bane, Jr.
Interior layout: Dustin Pickering
Cover design: AJ Price Design

FIRST EDITION

Acknowledgements

The poems in this volume appeared in: museumviews.com, Praxilla, The Calliope Nerve, Clutching At Straws, Back Room Live, The Indian Diary, The Indian Times. Word Pond, The Mondegreen, The Good Men Project, The Stockholm Review Of Literature, The Galway Review, Synaesthesia Magazine, Boston Poetry Magazine, Rain Party Disaster, Tincture Journal, Prism (Australia), The Journal (U.K.), Verse Wrights, Tinpahar Magazine, The Neglected Ratio, Vox Poetica, Strange Horizons, Tuck Magazine, Beatdom.com, SNR Review, The Camel Saloon, Poets Against War, Crack The Spine, Jab Magazine, Slice Of Solace, The Montucky Review, Kinship Of Rivers, Stepping Stones Magazine, eightyonefortynine.com, After The Pause, Hoax Magazine, Penwheel Lit, Similar Peaks, Origins Journal, Altar Journal, The Furious Gazelle, Snapping Twig, Bar None Group, Medium, Prick Of The Spindle, Mouth And Mouth Magazine, The Spiral Staircase, Makata, The Second Achilles, Jaded Ibis Productions, Spontaneity, The Magic Room Project, Basilica Press, Contemporary Literary Review India, Word Soup, One Throne Magazine and The First Literary Review East. My deep thanks to their editors.

Special thanks to Victor Giron at Curbside Splendor and Karen Kelsey at Aldrich Books for permitting us to reprint *The Chapbook* and *Love Poems*, respectively.

Finally, many thanks to Adriana Babiak-Vasquez and Luis Vasquez, Troy Camplin, Elina Petrova and Chris Juravich, Suzanne Denson, Charles Darnell, and Sarah Frances Moran. Without them, this book would not have been possible.

For Ann

Table of Contents

Acknowledgements..3

Dedication..5

    INTRODUCTION: LETTER TO RICHARD WILBUR......................................11

The Chapbook...13

    MY LOVE'S SWEET..13
    FIRE..14
    THE TWO...15
    MODO DE DIRE..16
    PICASSO'S GUITAR...16
    WE TROOPED INTO COUNTRYSIDE..17
    ALEXANDER'S SEIZURE..18
    WHEN SOMETHING CLOSES IN...19
    HOMELESS VET ON CONGRESS AVENUE.......................................20
    I MUST WRITE...22
    YOU...23
    MY OLD SOUL...24
    IN THE HOTEL...25
    MOTHER AND FATHER..26
    COME, BELOVED..27

Love Poems..28

    IN PARIS..28
    FOREVER NOW AND ALL I MIGHT HAVE......................................29
    FOR MY SON...30
    TWO..31
    FOR E.E. CUMMINGS..32
    I ONLY ARRIVED..33
    LET IT CUT...33
    YOU A CERTAIN CHORD...34
    WHEN I DESPAIR...35
    THERE IS..36
    WHAT I WHISPER..36
    AS EINSTEIN PEDALED..37
    UNDYING LIGHT..38
    AT THE OBSERVATORY..39

New Poems 40

    Hunting With Masai 40
    Thunder, Lightning 41
    Juan And His Wife 43
    When Masai Raise Spearheads 45
    Anzio 46
    Bronx Song 47
    I Am So Afraid Of Sleep 48
    How Long? 49
    What Rose Wanted 50
    All The Men Went 51
    And Then At Times 53

Author's Bio 55

The Ends of the Earth:

Collected Poems

Charles Bane, Jr.

Introduction: Letter To Richard Wilbur

Dear Richard:

It is dawn here on a Saturday morning in Florida, where I'm never cold. I can write as now on my terrace in almost every weather. And I'm visited throughout the day by many birds and once by a fox who clambered up and who I fed and watched sunning himself as I typed. I was far away, in the deeps of the unconscious, vast and ablaze: in the morning it mirrors the fortunes of the world, and it's open-lighted like the Globe. I climb its sheerest face and stand before creation everlasting, unfolded in a circle about a single star. I can only stay a short time before surfacing in a stream. When I return, my wife is making lunch. I return at night when the house is asleep.

I find words in the dark for the use of which I'm prepared to fall and though I thought once that I sensed some shadow in a room where I'd stopped and worked all night, I know it's no one greater than myself in the mirror of another cosmos neighboring ours. It is the same poetry that connects the two. It was a poem that was the singularity that strung galaxies like lyres, and in all poetry is a repair and inexhaustible tenderness identical to the one who reads.

Fingers of light appear when I'm finished working and my wife is awake, asks if I'd like to go out for coffee and I say certainly.

Charles

The Chapbook

My Love's Sweet

My love's sweet,
dreams are where we
must meet to soothe
the ache of lonely ties,
but are they not a finer
place? What is the sun?
A common turn of flaxen
thread, scattering wastes
overhead that weather conscious
life. But at twilight, love, the
flooring's swept, the loom
removed in lowering steps,
and a hearth of sparks is
overturned. In transit hours
I know unfailing life. Did we
not walk in reverie an Eden
of the evening long? Did we
not halt at an airy cataract and
naked in rapture, press our
lips below its spill? Do I not
love you well who carries from
his sleep an odor of stars?

Fire

Fire touches fire and in
the meeting is put out
til morning when we, in bed,
watch it rising from the east.
Such are we and all,
Other, from the ticking of
the first star. And all about
is rounded and curved that
we might find a pathway home.
All is made for but a little time
of light, and the light itself fashioned
by love for blazing kind. Here is
the truth, Other, that I read in my
twin's eyes: this space is all,
this patch for us between dark
and innocent dark. This waiting bed,
these sheets, this torch I hold. Fire
comes to fire, and mimics first light.

The Two

I think when God
walked shy to Moses,
stars clustered in his hands,
he led our rabbi down
to the orchards of the heart.
The two walked near the other
and traded dreams like brothers
before sleep. They paused
afield and watched the sun,
lifted by themselves in unison,
race overhead. And Moses knew
not to disappoint this man
with faltering steps or speech.
God wept uncomprehending
of his artistry and Moses scratched
some lines in stone to honor
a beloved friend.

Modo De Dire

Michelangelo cannot catch his breath. He
says nothing to his companions. How do you
say, the dust is numberless lights that fall
in fiery trails on clothes and hair and moving
hands? How do you say I labor here as the Maker
made, in shrift, a whole that echoes in my
every strike, and bathes my face
in rain? My hands move
in dreams I cannot show. Go home,
take wine. My neck lies on David's like a brother.

Picasso's Guitar

is disassembled and rebuilt
on canvas when figs are sugared
and clustered in the heavens and the studio
is silent; he makes short work of it,
and in the morning gives it only a passing
glance as it lays under a window and a dovecot.
He reaches instead to paint horses yellow and blue
that are streaming up a hillside like smoke, and when he
stops to look past the guitar and through the window
the fruit and birds are one.

We Trooped Into Countryside

We trooped into countryside,
walking behind tanks like children
trailing parents to a scene of petty
wrong. i was more exhausted
than I can say; I was tired of shots
and the substitute of guns for
the soundings of the sky and handsome
forks of gold like those back home
where storms are welcome to the eye.
This was a naked place, powdered
everywhere with dust and ash. It lay
on trees and covered men I shot
like birds and who dropped a little
spell away. At home,
the cathedral of the night
catches in its hands
our talk sometimes and you hear
the flight of the unseen
to firesides they crave.

Alexander's Seizure

It is an aloneness, this malady.
It hurled me from Bucephalus yesterday.
I fell (as I lay and shook
upon the fields) into the sea. There are always
dolphins waiting; in beautiful depths
I take a fin and watch patterns cross
the bodies of my companions that are cut from cloaks
of waves into handsome shields. I wish the world
was water. Swords are only flashing schools,
motioning past. The dolphins turned
to shallows and I cried, but made only bubbles.
I could not call, "Away from war. I watched you swim
at twilight once, and looked on peace."

When Something Closes In

When something closes in
that changes or seems
to change the prospects
of the day, I think of you
and your voice on the phone.
I hear waves of you returned
from space in sound that circles
half in dark, half in light to find
my waiting call. Baby, you say
and I take my cell outside and
standing, lift my face.

Homeless Vet On Congress Avenue

I can see that when traffic at your corner's stopped,
and flashing lights in blue and red signal the arrival
of our escort, you will be disconcerted;
soon, an altar boy will be beside you
and staring down at his calm face, you will calm in turn.
We must arrive at the basilica at the perfect light of day,
the perfect honored hour. Of all waiting inside, not one
does not feel a hollow and a fear that he or she will fail.
They bend in arcs of grace as doors open to ceremony
and looks from a country foreign to your every day
flood the interior. This is gallantry of forgotten kind to you,
beloved of me, who slept in viaduct and were rolled
by boys who made you curse. Rain halted fitful sleep.
Coins of light showering down make known what is put away.
Music rains on nave and aisle as even on the sunniest day.
Does it not halt your walk with speech that gives more than we,
all those times we sped as you stood bare?
Does it not make a hundred baths for a thousand lonely days?
Step and step forward once again, for it you wake them I too,
I swear, will slay the light that lies. You much reach the apse.
You must reflect windows more bejeweled than these,
if we are not to perish in the dark and refire in your mercy.
We await you at the front, we teem beside columns
and pictured scenes of sacrifice pale and unworthy
of modern pain.

Step and step again with boys long practiced in procession.
Forgiveness is the only faith worth wearing as a vestment.
Reach the dome, turn and say, Dona Nobis Pacem.

I Must Write

I must write to you; no,
that is not right. I must
take you to myself, a child
who speaks of pleasures
you have never known:
looking through a sextant
and seeing at my feet a length
of rope, coiling like the sun. Shall
I say we were once becalmed
until the wind fell upon our sails
like your lovely hands and we
struck for home? Is it
possible that in the garden you
could not feel the passing of yourself
like a Creator before
the only man to view
that loving face? It is a wonder
to a mariner that longitudes
can be erased and the bounty
of the earth heaped inside
my arms. My dearest, I must
embark; I send this on
other feet. I will pace
upon the roiling sea and think
that islands rising in the dawn
and winging friends from shore

are signals of your lift of me
from dust to follow
in your wake.

You

I came upon you
when I was a child
and kept the memory
close, through every
feverish year. My hair
was silk from corn; yours,
black as the birds upon the snow
I fed the winter long. I opened books
at night and looked at barest
trees and wished for Spring. I watched
for leaves birthing like the stars. I made
poems, and saved the lights I found
waiting in my marrow. One day I would tell
you of the music I heard between its honey-
combs and followed til words rested
on a page. You would understand. You
would hold the glass and pour my amber
work until it filled you to a brim.
You would say, this flames the trees
and you are the harvester of my soul.

My Old Soul

My old soul has sung before.
It has lain many hands in mine;
I reach for yours, and link it to he
who needs. He stands in Bergen-
Belsen in the rain, waiting his turn
to expire. He takes hands he cannot
save and sighs and breathes
the gas. He is a petal;
I see inside his heart. I love you as
he and they who follow down
the stairs. My hand takes yours and hers
and his. Be careful of their souls, they
are little suns. They rise in me and flame
the sanctuary where we stand, betrothed.

In The Hotel

In the hotel, unlocking
doors of time and space,
I knew we were met when
each was newly made. I knew
the laws were dust like dying
stars and worshipers lifting scrolls,
jeweled and dressed, are blind.
My love, I follow until the expiration
of the sun; my grail lays sleeping
far away and turns her head
alone; but an arc of burning dreams
hurries hours away and lashes
the horses of our wait.

Mother And Father

I dreamt of you together
in a sunny field, walking
to me, smiling. Is this true? Do
you pass from hand to hand what
here falls in common light? Is this
within your power? Mother, do you
kiss the necks of bathing souls and laugh
when you lower your Brownie? Are there
trains and trips to the city, and Mother,
is there refinement befitting such as you?
Did you find Ollie? Weep and brush his shoulder,
and tell him when he was downed you were crushed like paper?
Tell me you are there. Tell me you keep heaven coins
Dad would lose and spot clouds parting the horizon. Tell
me my beloveds, does innocence crowd you round
as we did all? Part, Mother, as boys did in Forest Hills
when you walked, smiling, to the subway entrance,
unbelieving you lived near?
Beloveds, we are well: life is Spring unsoiled in those
of us you carried.

Come, Beloved

I am hungry; come soon. I looked
tonight at flames like you upon
the west and jewels winging
home. I hold you in my eyes
when I see what cannot
be stamped again. All the earth
is of a kind but for the rarities
that clamber unknowing of their
gifts on vales of purest light,
and look at the common life
of us in shade. Come beloved,
soon.

Love Poems

In Paris

In Paris, all the streets
were rained and magpies
in the shadows of Notre Dame
poured tunes. The cafes dripped
and all the city was wet that
afternoon; you said, look
at the long haired Seine; do you want
to walk in the Jardins des Plantes ?
No, I said, let's hold Mass in your room.
You lay and I heard bells at the lifting
of the moon. A thousand souls somewhere
in the dark of France flew.

Forever Now And All I Might Have

Forever now and all I might have
been. I have never loved like
this. Never everything. Never from
town to town, or where I lay asleep,
or my hand straight and deer watching
as they take, hollowed before dark
and venturing to where day breaks.

For My Son

I will not waiver or protest
that the wait is hard to bear;
The parent to be is patient
for the child he cannot see, knowing
that eternity is rounding unknown
seas to fishing nets. My
beloved, I wait. I stand upon
the beach, my arms are wide, you
must swim to the sound of me
and lights undreamed. We shall be
coins of sides alike and sleep together
in the shade. You are the growing
length of me that lays
upon a floor of carpet leaves
and says, there is no end to light
or closing of the day. There are only
clarions that pierce the dark
with mirror songs like these.

Two

It defies logic so
Beautifully, this love.

Fall my love and I will
Rake the leaves

For e.e. cummings

Fleeter be they than dappled
dreams, and every word for
Marion is such and every day;
when I was lean and long
and words scraped against
the city skies of pages one
foot high, I raced in swimming
meets; the whistle blew and
I churned, arms winding like second
hands but really my joy propelled
me down the aisle as I thought
that time was not like her who I
would immortalize like air.

I Only Arrived

I only arrived from Mombasa
late last night and saw the city
raise her arms in lights, and
I hurried down the Champs
Elysses to meet you in the Parc
Monceau and all the lamps said
she is there, lifting what we do
not know.

Let It Cut

Let it cut deeper
love, until it flows
inside the blood.

You A Certain Chord

You a certain chord or
movement of a dance as
you crash in a tide and spill
like music or drugs into blood
and we down onto sheets,
your hair in kapok roots and
I think what bird is this, with
wings outspread, crying under
me?

When I Despair

When I despair, I hold
to you, the you that
cannot imagine floes or
among the masses one sees
everyday pained in
newspaper photos, the loss
of all. What can't be
endured is separation
I write, but you are my
religion too and I think
if the world could only glimpse
one face, all would be remade.
Is this not so? Can we walk with
all the population on the boulevards,
and lay all together with our
hands across our chests, looking
at the stars?

There Is

There is no
nothing as I
sleep inside
your soul.

What I Whisper

What I whisper
is not single celled,
but a colony and trees
bent in light leaving from
their stems wash the depths
of me. I am stunned when
morning comes; dew beads
every blade, and we who
loved the night shadows
are painted green.

As Einstein Pedaled

As Einstein pedaled his

bicycle in wide and wider arcs

and laughed among the multitudes

of pi, did he sense what

you and I discovered too,

that there is a great unsaid

and you alone with me walk the wildness

of its storms? Its circumference is garlanded

around your head and granaries

of unborn stars are sifted through the

hands, and my love, I fall.

I fall.

I fall unbordered, and

unwound as time

and surrounding like snow.

Undying Light

Undying light, undying
words that carry into
times to come the
power of undying such as
we, who loved and
fell . Spilling like
wine from the largest
skins, or clouds holding
seas. Beloved, all the
surface wears away the
stones of fear that stand
in the way of running
streams and the cupped
hands of explorers drink
cold and thirsty when
they kneel. Only mystics
see, but the air is charged
and forked and I have always
known what is written in
me is you, again and
again, repeatedly.

At The Observatory

At the observatory, I can
watch all the water mills
of galaxies. I deny every
injury in me and long to see
not backward but to forward
cliffs. I think the consequence
of you is written into the structures
we cannot know but by candles
in our room. Do you unfurl for
me? No, rather it is starry in your
eyes naturally and I want you
to order all the murdering
unstained from paper histories.
I deny sacredness
not born of your womb,
your hair the thousand
gestures of lovingness that
fall in gravity.

New Poems

Hunting With Masai

Dawn is spear and
shield and gun recklessly
left behind. We move in a
single line. Last night
they chased away a
missionary and we lay.
Mine is the god of the Hebrews
I explained, mountain born
like N'gai. He is not desirous
of you and only one
of mine has seen his face.
His mountain had boiled gravely
and he built a vessel of lava
rock for a climber overcome
to voyage fire home.

Thunder, Lightning

Thunder, lightning appear
on the sea and we slip to
Lesbos to be islanded and
enclosed.

Thunder, lightning. You roar
as I strike between your sandy
legs and we weep for the
banishment of emptiness
on the returning ship to
Athens streets.
Shall I lay my legs on
yours as we impregnate
the other eternally,
and birth from our lips
as we destroy our single
being, a crying child?

Thunder, lightning. I flash
behind your steps, unable
to describe on papyrus
the instance you slipped
into my menstrual flow
to heal small cuts and make my
heart beat longer for you
or your baths in the
sea that stirred me to compose
in the dark. Thunder
and lightning. I do not hate
men but how can I be tender
when every animal seeks out its
kind? Shall a bird love
shells or make nests for
hawks designed for doves?
Thunder, lightning are hammer
and necklace and we will never
return to any avenues but
their skies.

Juan And His Wife

Husband and wife were not
here legally, but Juan had
work at a market owned by
his kind and was far away
the strongest, most honest
hand. And to his wife he was
the man who would impale
her on his penis and walk with
her body wrapped round his
frame and speak to her like
a fawn. She kept a distance
from him, for respect.
Every day was a contest at
work of endurance; to catch
melon after melon from a truck
in the baking heat and when
he could take no more he
plunged his head into a barrel
of water and ice the owner kept
out of sight. Out of sight always
are the poor, except to the police
who knew Juan but looked the
other way. The police, Juan told
his wife as he wrapped her body
around his waist, are a covering
and your wavy hair knotted beads

the faithful hold when they stand
before divinity. They lay, and
Juan said more: you travel with
me constantly when I cross the
porous border of sleep. It was
with you I walked in the
coolness of early night as
the stars were named. Your body
that I'm entering was spotted there
and moon flaked and we were
alone as now without ownership of
anything but immortal ways.

When Masai Raise Spearheads

When Masai raise
spearheads to Ngai
at his falling wordless
leave, they mirror unsheathed
swords of city heights, wavering
in the breath of the unseen.
All mystery is powerless
before the respiratory fate
of light as you wash your
face, your back to me.
It is time to admit, as
I brush sand from
your feet, the odds
that a universe dimmed
will draw you in again for release.
You will be lost as four hundred
planets at first count are waterless,
or put in safekeeping of molecular cloud.
Somewhere distant, I will be noble
gas or fleeting charge. We will
meet, but incorporeal as gods.

Anzio

Oh they were alive
and playing cards
in an eight foot trench
that was covered like
Eve and I had point
alone on our Italian beach.
The Germans had artillery
so reaching that grunts robbed
of rest - all of them-
might disappear unclaimed
for weeks. I caught a private
and brought him back at dawn.
The captain said, take him there
behind those trees and hurry back.
To kill like that. I marched
behind the bastard and he knew
and wept. I was seeing things
from lack of sleep. I saw my father standing
on the platform by my returning train,
the haunted question of him; I saw
stars on collars finally unpinned
and the manual of arms above our
barn filled with grain. The German
knelt and light specked him unfed
and leather hooved. There were leaves
and I was dappled too.

Bronx Song

I wanna be wich you. By the chain
link fence on the corner we
walked past (where I kissed
u when u stopped and looked at me
and went, Dude). There was a street lamp
shining through the fence
onto a skip of oil
and somethin turned around.
Then I came home,
now thinking about u.
U stepping into day. On Sunday,
when even the Korean people
are a little nice. When the cooking
smells are horns. Hey, you know
that red like the truck outside
Schwartz's on flower day? That's
the red I wanna see u in and you
know and hey, that smell
when we were close, you buy
that at the store?
I saw your Mom there
and I go, Miz Hernandez , lemme
carry those and we walked
to your place and I look up
and your Mom goes,
love, it's like guava.

I Am So Afraid Of Sleep

I am so afraid
of sleep then
I remember a
hiking trip alone
and sheltering below
a ledge of stars.
So much dust
must constitute, I thought,
a comb for the lips of
yeshiva boys or an
interior of ascending
steps to the "Himalayas
of the soul". My night
watch was met by a band
of Perseids straddling
roofs and trees. Science
thinks particles are
scurrying from universe to
universe and when caught
in traps and released, they
leave fields of littered
interstellar shells and the
gravity of stamping feet;
they outline unnumbered game
deep in wilds of river stars. I
wanted to provision my

birch canoe, sweep their banks
and fire signals to their boundary
of our eastern dawns.

How Long?

How long since we changed the oil?
When I seizure, I'm confused. I
never told a soul until I met you. I was
afraid of small town rule; by force
of will, I begged sometimes to be
excused. Grand mal, you said, it
sounds so lovely; it sounds like
a painting Sargent might make
of Venetian canals. Let's walk,
you said, starling, and if
you drop, I'll stop mid-
flight to dip in foam.

What Rose Wanted

What Rose wanted
was for me to land
with my crew, racing
to her in the stealth
of night to bring
her fast to our boats.
She wanted Mass
in chapel the next
day and jeweled
windows braiding colors
across her face. She
wanted bright torches
of me and the flames
of every star. Look, she
said, they go to conquer
some army like themselves
in night fields far. Conquer
me, she said, make me
Crusade.

All The Men Went

All the men went
to the mines and
my grandfather carried
a canary in a small cage.
When the bird expired he
chose to stay as the others
rushed to air.
At his funeral Mass in
the church he never
entered, a choir sang
Danny Boy that was his
drinking song. No one
understood his choice
to lay beside his pick
and sleep; but I had
spent a night in his home
when I was small and called
down for his company.
He lay beside me
and explained how
the light that reflects
through a prism is a true
division of a miracle and
this was joyous to him to
know and he described
the tracks of carts carrying coal

and the flashing lamps of fellow
gods and he recounted, touching
my hair, the Iliad and Apollo of the sky
on a knee, firing arrows in single
beams.
He was without vice: but when the
elevator ascended from the shaft
in daylight savings time, grand-
mother told me he disappeared to
land for sale and tasted the rich black
soil of Illinois with a spoon. I think,
and write, of ultra violet and infra red
light that vibrates in every kind of
molecule, even cloud drops, in
a music for grandfather and choice
mythology.

And Then At Times

And then at times
the dips of our marriage are
no different than the falling
into love in Richmond Park
before we started home, and I
wrote every day until the motion
of the ship made me certain that
for every berth going out,
new souls put in, spit from
foam. If I could read Greek or
understand the errand of the
cardinal we watch for with coffee
in our hands, I could make poetry
on the tips of fence spears where
he stops and the fire of you would
go urgently from land to land.

Author's Bio

Charles Bane, Jr. is the author of *The Chapbook* (Curbside Splendor), *Love Poems* (Aldrich Press), and *Three Seasons: Writing Donald Hall* (Collection of Houghton Library, Harvard University). He created and contributes to The Meaning Of Poetry series for The Gutenberg Project, and is a current nominee as Poet Laureate of Florida.

Visit his website at www.charlesbanejr.com.

www.ingramcontent.com/pod-product-compliance
Lightning Source LLC
Chambersburg PA
CBHW070552300426
44113CB00011B/1883